C(

TRAVEL GUIDE

FOR

2023, 2024, AND BEYOND

**A Guidebook to
this Beautiful Country**

ALEXANDER HARRIS

TABLE OF CONTENTS

COLOMBIA

STATISTICS

Size: 1,141,748 square kilometers

Population: 50,339,443

Language: Spanish

Religion: Christianity

Top exports: Bananas, coffee, roses, and sugar

National anthem: "¡Oh Gloria Inmarcesible!"

Motto: Liberty and Order

National sport: Tejo

National tree: Wax Palm Tree

National flower: Cattleya trianae (orchid)

Currency: Colombian pesos

Capital city: Bogota

Land area: 1,038,700 sq km

Water area: 100,210 sq km

Border countries: Equator, Peru, Brazil, Venezuela, and Panama

Ethnic groups: 87.58% White-Mestizo, 6.68% Afro-Colombians, 4.31% Indigenous

INTRODUCTION

Colombia is one of the most culturally and geographically diverse countries in the world. There are over 87 indigenous groups and 65 different languages spoken here. This magnificent country is broken up into 5 different geographical regions with a large number of endemic species of flora and fauna. You can see the beautiful Pacific coastline in the west, the crystal clear Caribbean Sea in the north, three large mountain ranges in the center, savannas in the east, and the Amazon rainforest in the south.

With all of this variety, there is something to see and do for every type of traveler. Whether you are an adventure tourist, looking to surf the waves, or snorkel in Cartagena's crystal depths. Or, you are a family taking a relaxing vacation, sightseeing, and learning about the rich Colombian culture. Or, you are a group of young college students, looking to spend a fun-filled spring break in the sun. You can find a city for you.

Colombia is full of music, art, history, and adventure. The varied landscape paved the way to a variety of sounds, sights, and creativity in this county. You can see this in the colors of the buildings, the architecture, and the clothes people wear. Everywhere you look, there is vibrancy and color. This began with the early indigenous tribes and continues to the world-renowned musicians, artists, and writers of today. You can experience the creativity of the Colombian people in the local museums, along the streets, and in the instruments that play as you dance along an avenue.

The warm, springlike temperatures make beautiful Colombia a perfect place to vacation any time of year. The country has something to offer every month of the year, such as when a popular festival like Barranquilla's Carnival or Cartagena's Hay Festival is going on. But, these festivals are not the limits to the fun to be had within Colombia's borders. The country is teeming with delicious food to eat, unforgettable drinks, and nightlife that will get your heart pumping.

Nature lovers are not disappointed when they visit awe-inspiring Colombia. You can take a hike and walk the winding trails in many parks and preserves, which strive daily to preserve this fragile ecosystem from extensive cattle ranching and deforestation. These parks house species of plants and animals found nowhere else in the world. Hidden amongst groves and in underbrush are more animals to be discovered, as this is one of the most densely diverse locations for species in the world.

For travelers looking to bask in the sun on the beaches, there are several beautiful playas in Colombia. These beaches offer a chance for you to scuba dive, snorkel, swim, surf, wake board, water ski, sunbathe, or ride a boat in some of the most delightful waters in the world, since you can see both the Pacific Ocean and the Caribbean Sea in the same country.

You can also trek through the mountains, taking a look at some of the tallest and most active volcanoes in the world. You can also see ravishing waterfalls, crater lakes, and lagoons that have been untouched for thousands of years.

If you want a glimpse into the past, you can explore the tropical rainforest, where tribes of people live much as they have for hundreds of years. The jungle is a wild, untamed land, teeming with some of the most unique species of plants and animals on earth.

But nature isn't the only place to be in Colombia; the largest cities in this country are some of the most modern and forward-thinking ones in South America. You can enjoy skyscrapers, live music, crowds of exciting people, and breathtaking architecture in any of Colombia's largest cities.

Whether you plan to spend a couple of days or a couple of weeks, Colombia is a place where you can live life to its fullest.

Fun Facts

about Colombia

1. Colombia is home to the second-largest Spanish-speaking country in the world.
2. Colombia is named after the Italian explorer Christopher Columbus.
3. Radios and TV stations are mandated to play the national anthem every day at 6 a.m. and 6 p.m.
4. Although coffee is Colombia's number one export, the coffee tree is not native to Colombia.
5. Colombia has 18 national holidays, which is the second-largest number in the world.
6. The largest theater festival, the Iberoamericana, occurs in Colombia.
7. Colombia lies on the Ring of Fire and has 15 volcanoes.
8. Colombia has a free-market economy.

9. Colombia has a hierarchical society where people earn status through age and position.
10. La Quinceanera is a big event for 15-year-old girls in this country.
11. Shaking both hands is a custom for greeting someone and saying farewell.
12. People are encouraged to marry within their classes.
13. Colombians use both their maternal and paternal surnames.
14. This country is the second most biodiverse country in the world.
15. Colombia is number one in emerald exports in the world.
16. Colombia has a rainbow river that glows in red, blue, orange, yellow, and green due to algae.
17. Colombia has the 2nd largest Carnival celebration in the world.
18. There are 102 indigenous groups in Colombia.
19. Shakira is a popular singer who comes from Colombia.
20. There are over 60 national parks in the country.
21. The deserts in the northern part of Colombia have red rocks that resemble moon rocks.
22. Children, as well as adults, drink coffee.

23. The longest bicycle route in South America is located in Colombia.
24. Colombia has the world's tallest palm trees.
25. El Dorado was based on an indigenous man who lived in Colombia.
26. The Disney movie Encanto takes place in Colombia.

Brief History
of Colombia

Indigenous peoples lived in the Andes Mountain ranges along the Cordillera Oriental before the European conquest. Over one-third of the population was the Chibcha who lived in what is now the capital city of Bogota. The Chibcha people were trying to expand their control over other indigenous populations in the region through war, establishing chiefdoms with a central leader. The Chibcha and other indigenous Andean peoples were farmers and craftspeople. They had an organized religion, a system for class divisions, and for passing down offices through family lines.

The control of the Chibcha over the region was tenuous and war was ongoing, but they were beginning to unify when the Spanish arrived. In 1500, Rodrigo de Bastidas sailed the Caribbean coast of what is now Colombia. Francisco Pizarro sailed the Pacific coast of the country in 1525. That same year, Bastidas established

Santa Marta on the north coast. The other major cities shortly followed with Cartagena being founded in 1533 and Bogota in 1538. By 1549, the entire region was under Spanish control. A government was put into place.

By the 1600s, there was little left of the indigenous cultures. They were treated as slaves. Many intermarried with the Spanish and acclimated to the Spanish culture. The economy was fueled by mining and farming operations, as well as a textile industry north of Bogota.

The 1700s brought political changes. Spain was trying to centralize their control over their conquests while rebellions were brewing amongst the locals. By 1810, an uprising occurred in Bogota. Loyalties were divided between the crown and the separationists, and civil wars broke out. The Republic of Colombia was finally established in 1819. This region included what is now Colombia, Panama, Ecuador, and Venezuela. However, the other areas seceded from the union by 1835.

The 19th century was rife with civil wars, opposing political factions, and struggles between classes. Colombia refused the United States of America's offer to build a canal across the isthmus of Panama in 1903. The U.S. and Panama agreed to build the canal; however, that infuriated Colombia.

Then, Colombia adopted coffee as one of its major exports. Each decade, its coffee exports became more essential to the country's economy. Then, the depression hit in the 1930s and all of Colombia's major exports became devalued leading to an economic collapse.

After the economic crash, the Liberals came to power in Colombia. There was social, ethical, and industrial growth during this time. However, after World War II, a conservative was elected to power and a great political rift was created between the liberal and conservative parties. A liberal leader was assassinated in 1948 leading to a time dubbed La Violencia where feuding between the two parties reigned. During this time, Laureano Gomez tried to introduce a fascist regime to Colombia; however, that ended in a military coup.

Guillermo Leon Valencia became president in 1962. His presidency brought a decline in the peso and inflation. Marxist Guerrilla groups formed. Over the next few presidency terms, there was a back and forth between good strides and dissent. The guerrilla groups introduced a lot of violence to the region. Narcotics also became a problem.

Pablo Escobar formed a large-scale operation selling and exporting cocaine and other drugs out of the country. Violence still dominated the political landscape from the '60s through the '80s. In the 1990s, César Gaviria Trujillo tried to negotiate with the guerrilla groups and cracked down on drug trafficking; however, little progress was made, and violence still reigned.

In the early 2000s, the military made a move across Ecuador's borders, causing tensions. By 2002, violence had begun to settle down in the country. In 2017, an accord for a cease-fire had been signed with the government and the lead insurgent groups.

Today, Colombia is developing and recovering from some natural disasters and economic recession from the early 2000s. It has become a growing destination for tourism.

The Legend
of El Dorado

E l Dorado, or the lost city of gold, has long captivated the imaginations of people around the world. It is a tale of a city, completely made of gold, where this precious metal is as common as air, and everyone is draped in gold attire and jewelry.

The origin of the legend of El Dorado begins at Lake Guatavita, a little northeast of where Bogota now sits. The land in this area was sacred to the indigenous Muisca peoples from 600 to 1200 BCE. Here, a new king was crowned in an interesting ritual that led to the legend. The king would be taken to a cave and would be instructed to abstain from salt, women, and chili peppers. Then, he would offer up sacrifices to the gods to bless his reign. He would sit in the center of the crater-lake aboard a raft laden with gold and emerald treasures. They would also burn incense, which would fill the area with a mysterious smoke. The new king was stripped naked and covered in gold dust as part of the ritual. All of the people in attendance would throw gold jewelry into the lake as an offering. Then, he would jump into the lake and emerge cleansed of the gold dust.

Indigenous cultures in Colombia used gold for metalworking. It was not so much a currency as a material used for crafting. Gold was associated with the sun, and it was not a material limited to only the upper tiers of society, but also to the lower tiers. The Muiscas offered gold statues and artwork to their gods, and buried them in ancient rituals.

However, when the Spanish arrived, they were greedy, and gold was a symbol of wealth to Europeans. In fact, Spanish conquistadors were in active search of this precious metal. In 1531, when they arrived in the area, they knew about the legends of the lake. The conquistador, Gonzalo Jiménez de Quesada found the lake and began efforts to remove the riches from the sacred ground. They tried draining the lake and cutting a notch (which can still be seen today) into the lake. Each of the attempts reduced the level of the water, but hardened the mud beneath to make uncovering the riches impossible.

The legend of El Dorado was partially inspired by this lake and partially by the other stories told to the Spanish by natives. The Spanish were gold obsessed and only sought to conquer, destroy, and become rich. They did not understand the significance of these spaces, nor did they try to.

El Dorado may not have been a real city, but the gold work of the natives in Colombia can still be seen today in the Gold Museum and other museums around Colombia. The Muiscas have a rich and beautiful history that is worth checking out when you visit the country.

Today, many cities and excursions theme themselves off the El Dorado legend, so you will see a lot about the lost gold city on your travels to Colombia.

GEOGRAPHY

Colombia is the fifth largest country in South America. It is located in the northwest region of the country. Nicknamed the "gateway to South America," it is the only country in the continent attached to Central America.

The country is bordered by Panama to its north, Venezuela and Brazil to its east, and Peru and Ecuador to the southwest. Off the west coast, the country overlooks the Pacific Ocean. The northern water border is the Caribbean Sea.

The Andes Mountains run through the majority of the country. This range is split into 3 branches: The Cordillera Central (Central Range), Cordillera Oriental (Eastern Range), and Cordillera Occidental (Western Range). The Cuaca and Magdalena rivers run through these ranges and empty into the ocean.

The Cordillera Central is the tallest mountain range with snow-covered volcanoes reaching heights above 10,000 feet and above. The highest peak is Nevada de Huila, which is 17,602 feet.

The Cordillera Oriental is a much shorter mountain range with heights reaching no taller than 2,700 meters. There are several fertile basins here where there is rich farming and mining land. The nation's capital sits within this range.

Finally, in the Andes Mountain region, there is the Cordillera Occidental, which is located across the Cuaca Valley (a large rift separating the Central Range from the Western Range). This area has the richest farmland in the country.

In the north Caribbean lowlands, much of the banana and cotton are grown. This area has streams, swamps, and shallow lakes. There is an isolated mountain range with peaks of about 5,700 feet where cattle ranching often occurs.

On the coast of the Caribbean, Colombia is San Andres Island. This area is home to many bases used for science, military, and oceanography studies. Colombia lays claim to several islands in the Caribbean as well as two in the Pacific Ocean.

To the east of the mountains, savannas or "Los Llanas" dominate the landscape. There are many endemic species of vegetation in this region, but it is mostly used for cattle ranching and isn't very populated.

In the northwest region along the Caribbean coast, there is a jungle named "Choco" that goes through the Panama and Colombia border. On the Pacific coast, there are bays, inlets, and capes alongside sandy beaches.

The equator runs through the southern portion of the country. This is where the Amazon rainforest is located.

There are even deserts in Colombia. The Tatacoa Desert is in the Department of Huila. It was originally an area of lush and rich vegetation that has changed to desert land due to climate changes.

Another desert lies in north Colombia in the Department of La Guajira. It is the largest desert area in the region and is shared with Venezuela. The desert has large dunes and breathtaking landscapes.

The country of Colombia has a diverse geographical region with many interesting features and sights to see.

Departments of Colombia

Colombia is broken into 32 departments, each having its own governor and assembly. The departments in the north near the Caribbean Sea are the following:

- » La Guajira
- » Caesar
- » Magdalena
- » Atlantico
- » Bolivar
- » N. De Santander
- » Sucre
- » Cordoba
- » Antioquia

On the eastern side of the country, the departments are the following:

- » Boyaca
- » Arauca
- » Vichada
- » Guainía
- » Vaupes

To the south:

- » Amazonas
- » Punta Mayo
- » Caqueta
- » Guaviare
- » Narino

In the center of the country:

- » Meta
- » Huila
- » Tolima
- » Santander
- » Cundinamarca
- » Caldas

Finally, to the west of the country:

- » Cauca
- » Valle de Cauca
- » Choco

These municipalities work similarly to states, and have rotating elections every few years.

Endemic Animals

and Plants

Colombia has the third highest number of endemic (restricted to a certain space) species. The Amazon rainforest, Choco forest, Andes Mountains, and Andean savannas hold the largest number of these species both fauna and flora.

Animals

The country has over 200 species of bats, 260 species of carnivores, 38 species of primates, 105 species of amphibians, 27 species of turtles, and 2,000 species of fish.

Here is a list of some of the major endemic animal species you can find in Colombia:

Andean Condor

Condors have a wingspan of over 3 meters. They are some of the largest birds on the planet. Due to their large wingspan and heavy weight (about 30 pounds), they prefer to dwell where breezes are prevalent, such as the Andes Mountains. These largest birds feed on animal carcasses and occasionally steal eggs. A condor pair has only one baby every two years.

Spectacled Bear

Spectacled Bears are named so for the white marking around their eyes. They are the only bears found in South America. In Colombia, they live in Nevado del Ruiz, Purace National Park, and Chingaza National Park. These bears are extremely shy. They prefer cloud forests where they can climb upwards of 14,000 feet in the air to search for safety and vegetation to eat. They will, however, feast on insects, rodents, and small cows, as well.

Pink Dolphin

Pink Dolphins are 1 of 5 species of dolphins found in freshwater. These highly intelligent dolphins can be pink, as the name suggests, as well as gray and brown. The Pink Dolphins are friendly, and there are many legends amongst Amazonia tribes about them saving drowning humans and bringing them to shore.

Blue Anole

This pure blue lizard in the rainforests of the Pacific Ocean island, Gorgona Island, is very hard to find. Scientists do not know how many still survive in the wild. Their habitat has been severely reduced, and the introduction of predators threatens these rare lizards' survival.

Jaguar

Jaguars are six feet long with an additional 1 meter-long tail. They are the largest big cat in South America and hunt for fish and turtles by using their tails as a hook and dangling it in the water. They also leap at prey (typically capybaras, tapirs, and deer) to grab hold of them with their large mouth. This powerful bite is usually enough to take down the animal.

Plants

Colombia is such a biodiverse location. It is home to over 40,000 species of plants (about 10% of the world's plants). The country's wide variety of biomes creates environments for plants that are found nowhere else in the world.

Here are a few plant species endemic to Colombia:

Flor de Mayo Orchid

This tropical orchid grows up to 30 feet long and grows at heights of 2,000–3,000 meters above sea level in Cloud forests. This endangered species is the national flower of Colombia because the lip of the flower is yellow, blue, and red—like the Colombian flag. Flor de Mayo is a fragrant flower with leathery leaves.

Palma de Cera

In the Andes Mountains, the Palma de Cera towers to about 60 meters high. This is the largest monocot recorded. Its trunk is covered in wax, which is harvested along with the plant's fruit. The leaves, which are used in religious ceremonies, are dark green and grayish. The Colombian government has protection laws in place to preserve the plant since it was threatened due to overharvesting.

Marmalade Bush

The Marmalade Bush is a lush evergreen that produces inch-long yellow and orange trumpet flowers appearing year-round. These blooms attract birds and butterflies. The plant is located in the woodlands of Colombia. The bush is a rambler, so it needs heavy pruning to keep it in check, otherwise, it can grow around 15 feet high and 6 feet wide.

Encenillo Tree

At 15 to 25 meters high, this drought-tolerant tree grows in the Colombian Andes Mountain region. It has small, green leaves and cream-colored flowers. The Encenillo Tree has many uses. A substance is extracted from the tree and used for tanning leather to give it a shine. The tree can also be used for cheese preparation and timber.

CLIMATE

The lower half of Colombia is located at the equator, so most of the country remains at a constant temperature throughout the year. The upper half of Colombia is in the Northern Hemisphere while the lower half (mostly the Amazon basin) is in the Southern Hemisphere. There isn't a real distinction between seasons, but precipitation varies throughout the year.

The Amazon rainforest, Pacific coast, and Magdalena valley receive over 100 inches of rain and average temperatures of 74 °F. If you travel here, be sure to pack plenty of gear to tread through thick mud and standing water. It will be humid here, too, and the jungle will be swarming with insects. So, wear breathable clothing and bring bug spray.

In contrast, the southern Pacific coast, Caribbean coast, and Quindio department have a tropical monsoon climate. This means that the temperature averages around 68 °F. Around the winter solstice, there are a couple of drier months. The climate here is very comfortable, and great for beach-going. You should pack plenty of sunscreen, a bathing suit, light clothing, and bring a hat to ward off the intense sun.

There are tropical savanna conditions in the Llanos region. These have a long dry spell, usually from November to April, followed by a wet spell (May through October). The temperatures here average 74 °F, as well, with between 40–70 inches of rain annually. If you visit this region, prepare for the time you are visiting. During the dry season, you'll want more airy clothing and sun protection. During the wet season, you'll want boots, a hat, and a light jacket to ward off the constant rain.

In the northern part of the country, from the Gulf of Morrosquillo to the La Guajira Peninsula, it is much drier, and rain rarely goes above 30 inches a year. The temperature averages at about 81°F. Some areas of La Guajira reach desert conditions. This is a much hotter region. Make sure you pack plenty of light, breathable clothing, shoes to protect your feet from hot sand, sunscreen, a hat, and lots of water when visiting this region.

Finally, in the Andes Mountain region, where the majority of the population of the country dwells between the cordilleras. The temperatures in this area are cooler, decreasing as you go higher in elevation. The peaks of the mountains are perpetually snow-capped. In Bogota, one of the highest cities in South America, the temperatures average about 57 °F. It will be chilly here compared to the rest of the country; bring a light jacket and a few long sleeve outfits if you plan to stay along the cordilleras.

Although temperatures stay consistent throughout the year, the best time to visit Colombia depends on which part of the country you wish to visit.

In Bogota, April is a good time to visit. It is just before the busy season and right at the start of the rainy season. If you plan to visit Medellin, December through April is known for its springlike temperatures. December through March are the months to visit Cartagena for pleasant weather. Finally, if you plan to go toward Cali, the winter months are the best because of the city's drier weather and milder temperatures.

If you want to avoid crowds and don't mind the rain, you can visit Colombia during the off-season (September through November).

FOOD

The food in Colombia is one of the best reasons to visit the country. There are unique dishes for different regions. These dishes all have unique flavors and diverse ingredients. Some dishes are familiar and have made it into the mainstream and others are less common but just as appetizing.

Much of the country's population dwells in the mountain region, so many of the dishes there emphasize foods available in that area such as potatoes, dairy, beans, and beef from the cattle farming in the region. Guinea pig is a delicacy in this region. These dishes are also warmer and heartier because the Andes Mountains have cooler temperatures than other areas of the country.

Along the coastal region, meals showcase seafood such as shrimp, mussels, fish, and tropical fruits.

Colombians use a native herb that is somewhat similar to basil in many of their dishes. It is called guasca. They also use chives, annatto seeds, cumin, and cilantro.

Here are some foods you should seek out when you travel to Colombia:

Ajiaco

This is a chicken soup made with three kinds of potatoes (criolla, pastusa, and sabanera), corn on the cob, rice, chicken on the bone, cilantro, garlic, onions, and a local herb called guasca. The soup is a summertime favorite, traditionally topped with slices of avocado and sour cream. It originated from the city of Bogota in the Santa Fe region. Its warm heartiness is well suited to the cooler temperatures of the Andes Mountain region.

Arepas

Arepas are a popular street food in Colombia. They are bread made from corn and filled with cheese (arepas con queso) or eggs and meat (arepas con huevos). The arepas originated from the coastal region, in areas such as Cartagena and Barranquilla. You can eat this street food with any meal of the day.

Empanadas

This on-the-go fried food is a staple in Colombia. It has a cornmeal crust surrounding, traditionally, a filling of beef or pork and potato. However, the fillings are oftentimes regional. Colombians dip their empanadas in a sauce called hogao, which is a tomato paste and herb sauce. They also enjoy an aji sauce, which has garlic and peppers in it, with a slice of lime on the side. You can get empanadas pretty much anywhere in the country as street food or in local restaurants.

Arroz Atollado

Rice, pork, chicken, sausages, and potatoes with a hogao sauce make up this dish. It is often served with slices of avocado or hard-boiled eggs. This dish originates from the Valle de Cuaca region. It is a Colombian spin on risotto.

Tamales

Colombian tamales are a bit different from other tamales found in Central and South America. This street food is made with corn masa dough surrounding a beef or pork filling. They are usually cooked inside a corn husk. However, in Colombia, tamales may contain peas, potatoes, carrots, and chicken. They are boiled in banana leaves and served with a cup of chocolate.

Changua

A popular Colombian breakfast is a milk and water-based soup with green onions, cilantro, and parsley. Then, an egg is cracked into it as it cooks. It is often served either with arepas or stale bread. Changua used to be a way to eat stale bread. It is also considered a hangover cure. This soup hails from the mountain region where it is a favorite for holidays.

Bandeja Paisa

Known as the national dish of Colombia, Bandeja Paisa is a full breakfast with white rice, chorizo, red beans, plantain, chicharron (pork crackling), morcilla (a blood sausage), a fried egg, an arepa, minced beef, and a slice of avocado. This is served in a large portion. It is known colloquially as the "workman's platter." It originated in the Santa Fe and Medellin region. If you want to try this dish, you may want to share it with a friend.

Posta Negra

Originating in Cartagena, this dish has slow-cooked beef served on a bed of white rice or on fried plantains. It is drenched in a dark sauce made with Coca-Cola, Worcestershire sauce, onions, garlic, wine, cumin, brown sugar, and beef broth. This sauce is sweet and tangy. It is topped with fresh tomatoes and cilantro.

Cazuela de Mariscos

This Colombian seafood stew is made with coconut milk; a combination of mussels, clams, shrimp, oysters, squid, octopus, and white fish; pepper, tomato paste, white wine, butter, and seasonings. It is a popular dish for holidays and dinner parties. It hails from the coastal region where you can get plenty of fresh seafood locally. This is a thick stew popular in Cartagena.

Pastel de Gloria

If you are looking to try some of the sweets in Colombia, this is a tasty pastry filled with guava, cheese, and dulce de leche. They are bite-sized treats baked golden brown and served with a sprinkling of powdered sugar on top. They are a combination of sweet and salty.

Torta Envinada

This dessert is a cake made with spices, dried fruits, nuts, butter, flour, and eggs. The batter is given a caramel coloring and baked. Once it comes out of the oven, it is doused in red wine and left to sit for a couple of days. This cake is often eaten on holidays and on special occasions.

Pan Trenza

It is a traditional bread made from flour, eggs, oil, yeast, sugar, and salt. Guava, raisins, and cheese are often added to the dough. Once the dough is formed, it is rolled into strands and braided. Then, it is baked until it becomes golden brown. This delicious Colombian bread can be found in most local bakeries.

When you eat at a restaurant, you can expect a typical Colombian meal to consist of empanadas or fried plantains as an appetizer, soup, beans or rice with meat, and a fruity or milk dessert. Arepas are served with every meal.

DRINKS

When you visit Colombia, sampling the cuisine also includes the local drinks. Whether you want to taste the local alcoholic beverages or more tame thirst-quenchers, there are a lot of tasty drinks to try. You can get a variety of warm and cold beverages at local restaurants and bars.

Here are some delicious drinks to try when you visit Colombia:

Aguardiente

This alcohol is made from sugar, water, alcohol, and anise. Most bottles contain 29% alcohol content. Aguardiente is best paired with other flavors. It isn't a complex drink. The flavor doesn't change with age.

This alcoholic beverage is served either lukewarm as a shot or warmed with lime and cinnamon. Aguardiente is the national alcohol of Colombia. It is everywhere you look, and is a must-try on your trip.

Coffee

Although most of Colombia's best coffee beans are exported to other countries, the coffee is still worth trying. Many cafes are starting to keep some of the best beans to sell to tourists. You can pick up a tinta, or small cup, in towns where coffee is grown, but this is the worst quality coffee made from defective beans. Instead, choose to get a cup at a local cafe for better quality.

Champus

The drink is made with a mixture of ice, pineapple, naranjillas, dried corn, panela, cloves, and cinnamon. It is a cold drink from the Valle de Cauca department. It is popular for family get-togethers and holidays.

Chocolate con Queso

Hot chocolate with cheese in it is a delicious treat you can get in Colombia. Cheese is placed in the cup and the hot chocolate is poured over it. This creates a thick, heavy drink good enough for a snack. The drink is often paired with cinnamon and sugar to add sweetness.

Limonada de Coco

This cool and refreshing drink hails from the Coast, where it is a refreshment for those hot days on the beach. It is made from coconut milk, lime, ice, and sugar. Most local restaurants serve this tasty beverage.

Masato de Arroz

Unlike many of the other beverages available, this one is from before the Spanish colonization. Masato de Arroz hails from the Andean region. A fermented syrup of cloves and cinnamon is added to soft rice and corn, then the grains are strained, and the liquid is served over ice. It has a creamy texture and is usually accompanied by cookies. You can get this drink in the Tolima and Cundinamarca departments.

Colombian Soda

The most popular soda in Colombia is Postobon. It has a variety of flavors including lemon, pineapple, grape, and apple. Another brand called Pony sells root beer and Colombiana sells a cream soda flavor. These are pretty cheap and tasty drinks to try while on vacation.

Fruit Juices

At local mercados (outdoor markets), you can find a variety of local, tropical fruits and fruit juices. Lulo juice is made from a local fruit that is small and orange. This citrusy, tangy fruit is full of vitamins A and D. It is a delicious juice and healthy, too.

Guanabana is another local fruit. This fruit has a hard, green exterior with a white, creamy interior. It is often combined with milk. It tastes like a banana mixed with citrus fruit.

Another local fruit is Tamarillo. It is a small fruit in the shape of an egg. It can be red, orange, purple, or yellow. It is native to the Andean region. In texture, this fruit is much like a tomato, but it tastes tangier. The fruit juice is very delicious.

There are also many local beers and wines you can drink in Colombia. These can be found at local bars, restaurants, and breweries.

In addition, most of the tap water in Colombia is safe to drink, especially in places like Bogota, Medellin, Cartagena, and Cali. In smaller cities, if you notice the locals drinking purified water from a bottle instead, follow suit, as the water quality may not be good in these areas.

MUSIC

The diversity of Colombia's people is reflected in their folk music. Colombia is often called "the land of a thousand rhythms." Many of the songs and rhythms produced in this country are tied to dance. From town to town, these rhythms can vary, and the songs and dances can last hours or days long.

The instruments most commonly used in these songs are the following:

- » Kuisi (a.k.a. gaita) - a flute made from a cactus stem
- » Tambora - a two-headed drum often salvaged from rum barrels
- » Marimba - a set of wooden bars that are hit with a mallet to produce sound

These instruments are used to produce rhythms unique to the region from which they hail.

Along the Atlantic coast, **cumbia** originated. It is dance music with a complicated rhythm. The rhythm represents the sound of the shackles of the African and Indian slaves. Originally, it featured one singer with a percussive background, but the folk tradition has expanded since then and is played by big bands and listened to by other Latin countries.

Another Caribbean coast rhythm, **mapale**, originated in Africa. It has a fast rhythm composed mostly of clapping. Now, it is a fast dance performed by amorous couples.

Vallenato originated from an Atlantic coastal city called Valledupar. This genre contains four rhythms: Son, Puya, Merengue and Paseo. It features several instruments:

>> Three-row button accordion
>> Caja vallenata (box drum)
>> Two guitars
>> Tiple (a 12-stringed instrument)
>> Guacharaca scraper (a percussive instrument shaped like a gourd with holes in it)

The Pacific coast has **currulao**, a rhythm with Afro-Colombian origins that features the marimba.

Finally, the Andean mountains have **bambuco,** a duet or trio. The band plays a guitar, a mandolin, and sometimes a flute.

Besides traditional folk music, there is also contemporary Colombian music. Although it didn't originate in Colombia, Colombian salsa is a popular musical genre. Several popular performers in the genre come from Colombia. Also, the dance is different from Cuba salsa. The Colombian dance focuses more on footwork than body crosses. The upper body is still and relaxes. The feet do complex steps.

In Bogota, there is an annual event called "Rock al Parque," which is the largest Latin America rock festival. The event spans 3 days, has over 100 bands, and over 400,000 people in attendance. The festival features popular rock bands from across Latin America.

Pop music in Colombia has names you may recognize such as Shakira, Fanny Lu, Ilona, and Carlos Vives. Many of these singers combine popular sounds with traditional Colombian rhythms. They are usually performed in both English and Spanish.

Where can you visit to listen to the traditional and contemporary music of Colombia?

- » **Barranquilla -** If you visit during Carnival (usually in late February), you can experience many of the local sounds of the Caribbean region of Colombia.
- » **Cali -** This city is considered the Salsa Capital. You can go to local bars and dance clubs to dance salsa. Or, get formally trained with local dance lessons.
- » **Amazonas -** You can listen to traditional, ritualistic music while exploring the jungle and the local culture.

- » **Medellin -** You can check out the night clubs here for fun, dance music with a Colombian beat.
- » **Cartagena -** You can listen to the champeta music in this region as you explore the city streets.
- » **Villavicencio -** The rhythm joropo is played in this region. The sound incorporates maracas, the harp, and a cuatros guitar.

ART

Painters and Sculptors

Colombia has a beautiful and diverse art culture. Many people foster their creativity at universities and art schools across the country, however, there is no formal, national art school. There have been several famous Colombian artists who have made it to the international scene.

One of these artists is Fernando Botero, whose work you can see in big cities throughout Colombia. Botero does sculptures and paintings that feature disproportionate, inflated animals and human figures. Not only is Botero's work found throughout his home country, but you can also see figures in Park Avenue, New York and Champs-Elysees, Paris. Botero first exhibited his work in 1948. Now, he has over 50 exhibits worldwide.

There are several other notable artists from Colombia including the following:

» Alejandro Obregon (painter, sculptor, engraver, and muralist)
» David Manzur (award-winning painter for still lifes of knights and saints)
» Enrique Grau (famous for his depictions of Amerindians and Afro-Colombian figures)
» Omar Rayo (painter, sculptor, caricaturist, and plastic artist primarily working in geometric abstract art)

Writers

Other famous artists and art in Colombia include the works of Colombian author, Gabriel Garcia Marquez, who won the Nobel Prize for Literature in 1982. Marquez was born in Aracataca, Colombia in 1927. He wrote screenplays, short stories, novels, and news pieces. He was a significant Spanish writer who published works such as *One Hundred Years of Solitude* and *Love in the Time of Cholera*. These works received critical acclaim and commercial success. He was active politically throughout his life and inspired many young, Colombian writers to pursue a similar career. There are monuments to him throughout the major cities in the country.

Other famous writers include the following:

» Rafael Pombo (a romanticist poet and children's writer)

- » Jose Asuncion Silva (a modernist poet famous for "Nocturno")
- » Porfirio Barba Jacob (a poet famous for "Canción de la vida profunda")
- » Jorge Isaacs (a poet and novelist most famous for Maria: A South American Romance)
- » Gonzalo Arango (a poet, writer, and journalist who led the Nadaismo movement)
- » Jose Eustasio Rivera (a novelist known for The Vortex)
- » Leon de Greiff (a poet who used obscure lexicon in his works)

Fashion Designers

In addition to painters and writers, Colombia has some famous fashion designers amongst its artistic alum. The textile industry has long been an important part of Colombian culture. Weavers and artisans construct beautiful, vibrant clothes, blankets, and bags. Many indigenous tribes still weave yarn by hand to create exquisite works of art in fabric.

Because of this history, it is no surprise that fashion is important in Colombia. Many Colombian fashion designers are up and coming in the world of fashion.

For example, Johanna Ortiz, who grew up in Cali, creates skirts and tops representative of her salsa routes with close attention to the types of fabrics she uses. These styles are meant for women and represent joy and strength.

Maygel Coronel is a fashion designer who is making waves in swimwear. She uses ruffles, single-shoulder looks, and clean lines to create her signature look.

Another fashion designer named Diana Crump uses vivid colors to reflect the vibrancy of the lovely Colombian landscape and culture. Her trendy clothes embrace femininity with bold colors and patterns.

Other famous fashion designers include the following:

- » Maria Luisa Ortiz (a haute couture designer)
- » Kika Vargas (a designer who focuses on asymmetry and ruffles to create her signature looks)
- » Carlo Carrizosa (a designer who features handmade textiles in his designs)
- » Pink Filosofy (a designer who emphasizes femininity and contemporary looks for women)

Film Makers

Colombian artists are also famous for their films. Since Colombia has so many varied landscapes, filming in the country provides you with an array of settings to shoot. In fact, two recent filming laws were placed into effect to draw international movie-makers to the country. These laws incentivize filmmakers. One of the most recent critically acclaimed films out of Colombia is *El Piedra* by Rafael Martinez. The story follows a retired boxer who comes face to face with someone claiming to be his child. The kid wants to learn boxing, and the pair learn and grow throughout the film.

Another critically acclaimed film is *Killing Jesus* by Laura Mora. This film follows an undergraduate student, Paula, as she seeks revenge for her father's murder. The film takes place in Medellin.

Other famous filmmakers from Colombia include the following:

>> Andrés Baiz (famous for *Passing By, The Hidden Face, Penumbra, Satanás*)
>> Rodrigo García (famous for *Tired of Being Funny, Revolución, Fathers and Sons, Ten Tiny Love Stories, Passengers*)
>> Juan Manuel Echavarría (famous for *Dos Hermanos*)
>> Ciro Guerra (famous for *The Wandering Shadows, The Wind Journeys*)

SPORTS

The magnificent Colombia enjoys many different sports. The most popular sports are futbol, cycling, basketball, and baseball. To a lesser extent, those with more money enjoy golf, tennis, and volleyball. Another popular sport is automobile racing, which turns up large crowds each year. While in Colombia, if you are a sports' enthusiast, it would be fun to check out a game or two.

Soccer

The most popular is futbol (soccer), and this country has produced some of the best futbolers in the world. The national team has won Copa America 3 times and played in the World Cup twice.

You can visit the **Estadio Metropolitano Roberto Melendez** to catch a futbol game in the northern region of Colombia in Barranquilla. This stadium has the capacity to hold 50,000 spectators. The locals are passionate, and the stadium fills up fast.

Cycling

During early August, the **Vuelta a Colombia (Tour de Colombia)** occurs. This large, annual cycling race has several stages—some crossing into Ecuador and Venezuela. There are over 120 kilometers of roads. This takes place in Bogota each year. The unique terrain in fascinating Colombia provides cycling enthusiasts with a wide variety of challenging and exciting experiences. Many of the cyclists who come from Colombia are excellent. They are used to changes in altitude and steep roads.

If you are in Bogota during early August, it would be worth it to check out the Vuelta a Colombia—the locals will be!

Basketball

With over 3,000 teams, Colombia's interest in basketball is growing fast. Bogota has several basketball courts for people to play at. Locals and professionals alike can join in the fun. There have been some notable basketball athletes to come from Bogota. If you are in the region, you can check out one of the local courts for a quick game. It's fun and great exercise!

Baseball

Most of the major league baseball teams in radiant Colombia come from Cartagena a Barranquilla. Colombia is currently a powerhouse in baseball, defeating

US and Dominican Republic teams in recent games. The Caribbean coastal region prefers baseball to futbol, and shows up in droves to the games.

In 2018, the **Edgar Renteria National Baseball Stadium** was opened in Barranquilla. This large and impressive stadium can seat 12,000 spectators. It is a modern venue for locals and tourists to check out the competitive baseball teams along the Atlantic coast.

Car Racing

The **Autodromo de Tocancipa** in Bogotá is the only active motor racing circuit. In December, this venue hosts a six-hour endurance race. Not only can you catch a race here, but there are also a variety of other car experiences hosted at this venue, including:

- » Car shows
- » Drag races
- » Track days
- » TC 2000 touring days
- » Classic car events

If you love automobiles and car racing, check out this venue while you are in Bogota.

THE BEST BEACHES

With two beautiful ocean coasts and year-round spring-like temperatures, glamorous Colombia is a great destination for a beach trip. If you are looking to visit a beach while traveling to Colombia, check out the following beaches.

Pilon de Azucar

Along the Caribbean Sea where the Guajira Desert meets the sea, there is a beach with orange and red sands. The ocean is gentle and perfect for swimming. The shore is rocky and serene. The waters are sparkling. There is always a coastal breeze. You can get a view of the desert while also seeing the tall mountain ranges rise in the background. It's a truly breathtaking destination.

Playa Blanca

A little southwest of Cartagena, you can go to the Isla Baru. This peninsula is only accessible by boat, but the trek is worth it. On the peninsula, you can eat at the local restaurant, lounge in chairs, and relax as the waves roll to shore. This is a popular vacation spot located in the Utria National Park. During July through October, you can even catch a glimpse of humpback whales as they travel to their mating grounds.

Guachalito Beach

If you want a truly stunning and unique beach experience, Guachalito Beach is located on the Pacific coast in Choco National Park. This beach is located on the Gulf of Tribuga. This is a half-hour boat trip away from Nuqui. The jungle meets the ocean and beautiful waterfalls cascade into the sea along the dark sand of this beach. It is truly a magnificent sight.

Cabo San Juan

This beach is located inside the Tayrona National Park on the Caribbean side of the country. Cabo San Juan is a unique tourist beach experience. The beach has a scenic view. It is surrounded by plants, and there is a rocky hill in the middle with a cabin on top of it. The view from the cabin is one of the most spectacular in Colombia. The waters here are dazzling blue, and the landscape is breathtaking. To get to Cabo San Juan, you have two options: take a boat or hike 2–3 hours through the park. So, this beach takes some effort, but the payoff is worth the work. The park does have an entry fee, and the boat ride is usually around 15,000 COP. Once you get here, there are several camping sites in the area and a restaurant, so you could spend a day or more of your vacation here.

Taganga Beach

Taganga is a city 5 km north of Santa Marta. It is a common resting point for backpackers and a beautiful site with green mountains and a stunning bay. It is a small beach, but it is surrounded by lush, green mountains. The town itself has grown in the past few years. There are plenty of hotels, shops, and restaurants in this area. The waters are calm enough for swimming, and the bay affords a nice spot for scuba divers. The beach can get particularly busy during weekends, and there are some reports of crime rates rising over the past couple of years.

El Rodadero

Located in Santa Marta, this beach is located along the Caribbean coast. It is a popular tourist location. The city has bars, hotels, and restaurants for you to visit. The beach itself is sunny, and the water is perfect for swimming and water skiing. This beach can get busy, but it is a beautiful location with plenty to do.

Parks and Preserves

With radiant Colombia's incredible biodiversity, there are parks and preserves established to protect the endemic wildlife and plants. Many of the world's species dwell here in the rich landscape of this South American country. These parks are a beautiful homage to the country's natural wonders. They are a must-see when visiting Colombia.

Malpelo Flora and Fauna Sanctuary

Off the port of Buenaventura, Malpelo island is located about 500 km into the Pacific Ocean. This is the 9th largest protected marine area in the world. The location is also declared a World Heritage Site by UNESCO. The island is small, but it plays an important role in the reproduction of many marine species, including hammerhead sharks. The Sanctuary is a deep sea diver's dream. There are underwater caves, tunnels, and steep walls. There are hundreds of species of marine life dwelling amongst these rocks, including 5 that are endemic to Colombia. If you enjoy scuba diving, this is a spectacular destination to visit.

Utria National Natural Park

On the north Pacific coast of photogenic Colombia, the Utria Inlet is home to estuaries and mangrove swamps with the foothills of the mountains visible to the South. Marine turtles, migratory birds, and spawning fish find this place irresistible. Tropical forests surround the area. It is an idyllic landscape. The parks cover not only the land but the marine environment around the inlet. The park is run by local indigenous peoples. It can be reached by boat from Buenaventura, or you can trek from the village El Valle for 3 hours through the tropical forest to reach the park. There is a restaurant and meager accommodations once you reach your destination.

It is important to bring your ID and health records with you. People must be vaccinated for yellow fever and tetanus before traveling to this park.

Once you are in the park, you can walk through many of the trails, scuba dive, snorkel, swim, or relax on the local beach.

To keep this area pristine, there are several restrictions including:

» No pets
» No aerosols
» No alcohol
» No firearms
» No noise that would disturb wildlife
» Take your solid waste with you as you leave

Many beautiful plants found in this region are useful to the indigenous populations as food, crafts, and medicine. There are several animal species found in these forests including the jaguar, the white-lipped peccary, and the black-headed spider monkey. The forest has a high density of biodiversity.

If you want to see a natural spot in Colombia full of biodiversity and indigenous culture, this park is a worthwhile visit.

Uramba Bahia Malaga National Natural Park

This protected area is located in the mid-section of the Colombian Pacific Coast. The area includes 4 beaches with strong waves, a bay surrounded by rocks, and a dense forest. There are several islets inside the bay.

The national park is a great humpback whale-watching area. It is also a great bird-watching destination. There are no hotels or restaurants in the park, so pack a snack as you hike the trails and explore the diversity of the forest. It is recommended that you wear rubber boots and bring along insect spray for this hike. The humid forest can be muddy, and insects abound.

Isla de la Corota Flora and Fauna Sanctuary

In the Andean Mountains, you can visit this sanctuary that is shaped like a turtle shell emerging out of the water. This sanctuary is located near the Laguna de la Cocha. The sanctuary is located approximately 1.3 km from El Puerto by bus. You can observe the diverse flora and fauna in this location, hike the many trails, and take pictures of some beautiful landscapes.

Along one of the trails, you can visit the Virgin of Lourdes chapel, but the chapel has some structural weaknesses that make it a bit dangerous. The park officials advise you to only stay a short time in the chapel.

Once you finish hiking, you can visit restaurants and shops along the Laguna de la Cocha.

Parque Nacional Natural Tayrona

Located near Santa Marta, the Tayrona National Park is an ecotourist spot with mangroves, beaches, reefs, and Indian ruins. It is a large park with over 37,000 acres of natural beauty. This is a popular tourist destination, so it can get busy. Yet, there is so much to do here. There are lots of animals and plants to see. You can go horseback riding, snorkeling, scuba diving, camp, hike, rest by the beach, swim, and visit the ruins of Pueblito Chayrama. This location also has plenty of local vendors and restaurants you can visit.

Los Nevados

If you are a fit, adventure tourist, this park is for you. In the park is the extremely active volcano Nevada del Ruiz. Park officials advise you to check the status of the volcano before making a trek to this location. The snow-capped glaciers and rivers supply water around the region, trickling into tributaries, farmlands, and wetlands surrounding the park.

Condors, hummingbirds, tapirs, bears, and cougars live in this region. The flora and fauna are diverse and beautiful.

Much of the park is at a high altitude, so visitors are advised to only adventure here if they are in peak physical condition. The sun is strong, so UV protection is strongly advised. Sturdy footwear and appropriate clothing for colder temperatures are also a must.

Sierra Nevada del Cocuy National Park

In the Andes Mountains, along the Cordillera Oriental, sits this national park. It holds the largest glacial mass in South America. The glacier is said to look like a rosary of white pearls against the Andes. This park is home to an indigenous tribe called the U'wa. They hold this land as sacred, so the eastern side of the park is closed to tourism.

The park has 150 lagoons, several waterfalls, and rock faces you can visit. The chief activities in this park are hiking, rock climbing, and camping. There are several trails to traverse but check with the park administration upon arrival to learn which trails are open and which are closed. There are a couple of campsites you can stay at, as well. This is the perfect place for adrenaline junkies.

Chingaza National Park

If you are staying in Bogota, this park is only around 40 miles northeast. This park includes the paramo (Andes wetlands) that provide the capital's drinking water. There are over 60 glacial lakes and over 2,000 endemic species of flora and fauna to be found in this area.

Before planning a trip to the park, make sure to check with the park services. You need to make a request 15 days in advance before your visit. Also, some of the trails are limited to only 40 travelers at a time.

Because the park is so large, it is only possible to visit one sector of the park per day. So, you can take advantage of the campsite for longer stays.

There are 6 ecotourism trails, and each follows a certain theme. You can see the wonder of this natural environment. This is a great activity for bird watchers and nature lovers.

Chiribiquete National Park

The largest national park in Colombia protects 2,782,354 hectares of ecosystems. It sits in the confluence of the Amazon, Andes, Orinoco, and Guyana provinces. Amongst the sheer number of beautiful and endemic flora and fauna of this region, there are sandstone plateaus known as tepees that surround the area and offer it protection from the outside world.

In addition to the park's natural scenery, there are over 75,000 figures painted on rock walls by indigenous peoples dating as far back as 20,000 BCE.

This site is considered sacred ground and is completely off-limits to tourism, however, you can book a private flight to overlook this pristine park.

There are many other national parks in Colombia. No matter where you plan to stay, there is sure to be a park close by that you can visit and explore the natural beauty of the country.

The Amazon Rainforest

The Amazon rainforest passes through the departments of Amazonas, Putumayo, Caquetá, Guainía, Guaviare, Vaupés, Cauca, Meta, and Vichada. Within the forest, which surrounds the Amazon River. The river provides transportation and nutrients to the region. Many native communities live in this region. They live off the land and remain, relatively untouched by modern society.

The main indigenous tribes of the region are the ticunas, huitotos, and yucanas. These peoples' cultures are preserved by 185 reservations.

There are over 212 mammal species, 195 reptile species, and a variety of bird species. There are also famous pink dolphins who live in this region.

The jungle is also home to many types of plants, vines, flowers, and tall trees. Many of these plants have rich, medicinal value.

If you are interested in visiting the Amazon rainforest, you can explore the jungle through ecotourism. Ecotourism strives to bring this untouched forest within reach of curious visitors while also protecting the wonderful environment.

Adventurers can climb tall trees, hike the jungle, ride on zip lines, sail along the Amazon River, visit remote villages, try indigenous dishes, interact with the locals, and enjoy the natural beauty of the world around them.

The best time to visit the Amazon forest is between November to February. This is the time when the routes aren't too flooded to visit. The town of Leticia is close to the Peruvian and Brazilian borders. It is the easiest access point to explore the Amazon region.

It will take you approximately three days to get to Leticia. Since you are so close to the border, you can often pop over to Brazil and Peru for a quick visit, while you are in the area.

You will need to make sure you are up-to-date on your vaccinations before traveling to the Amazon rainforest. Also, bring plenty of bug spray. Mosquitos are abundant in the damp, humid forest. They can carry diseases, especially yellow fever, and malaria.

To get to Leticia, you'll need to travel by plane to the Vazquez Cabo Airport. You can take a taxi or walk for twenty minutes to get into the city from the airport. While in the city, walking will be your main mode of transportation. You can also take ferry boats or steamboats and explore the river.

There are several local hotels you can stay at and local eateries you can dine in. Once you are there, it is an adventurer's paradise, with plenty of things to see and experience around every corner.

You will not be in the lap of luxury, as in the big cities in Colombia. Wi-Fi and modern amenities may be hard to come by, but you will be able to see a region that is very much as it has been for hundreds of years.

FESTIVALS

I f you arrive in Colombia at certain times of the year, you may get to see some fun and interesting cultural festivals. These take place all over the country and give you a real glimpse into the culture and heart of Colombia. Listed below are some of the most popular festivals to attend.

Carnival de Barranquilla

If you are visiting Barranquilla in February, check out the second largest carnival festival in the world. Prior to the festival, the city begins to gear up for the celebration with parades starting in January.

The actual event spans four days, each dedicated to a different cultural, historical, or traditional event. These days will have dancing, music, and performances that will captivate your senses. The city is lively during this season. People eat, drink, dance, and enjoy the festivities together.

Festival Internacional de Cine de Cartagena

In March, Cartagena has the longest-running film festival. The event allows local cinematographers and filmmakers to show off their craft. This arena is the launching point for many Spanish actors, directors, and producers.

You can attend a screening of these films during this festival week at many of the outdoor locations in Cartagena. Most of these have free admission, but you do need to secure a ticket.

Vallenato Legend Festival

If you want to listen to the musical sounds of the Caribbean, this festival takes place in April in Valledupar. This festival pays homage to the troubadours who used to travel from town to town spreading news, music, and poetry.

It is a cultural festival with musicians of all levels playing vallenato music. Musicians even "showdown" in what is called the piqueria. This is an improvised musical performance in response to another musician.

You can enjoy these live concerts in the main square of the city.

Feria de las Flores

In Medellin in August, you can check out artwork made from flowers and plants. The event features a parade where silleteros (the artists of these plant sculptures) tote their creations on the backs. The silleteros' act is a symbolic representation of Santa Elena, a legendary figure who was said to have brought flowers down from the mountains on her way back to the city.

You can go by the Botanical Gardens to see a flower exhibit of the country's prized flowers. There is also an antique car show with outdoor concerts, workshops, and market vendors. The event is free of charge, but the crowds can sometimes be overwhelming. It is a fun, affordable event.

La Noches de la Faroles

To commemorate the immaculate conception of the Virgin Mary, the town Quimbaya holds this festival in December as part of the Dia de las Velitas. On this day, households will put decorative paper lanterns on their window sills with lit candles. Although this happens throughout the country, Quimbaya's neighborhoods compete by decorating their houses and candles very elaborately.

As you walk through the city, you can see the warm glow of the candles and the religious symbols depicted in the artistic lanterns and decorations.

Rock al Parque

One of the biggest free festivals in South America happens in Bogota in August. This largest outdoor rock concert venue attracts between 300,000–400,000 attendees each year. Rock artists from over 30 countries perform at the Plaza de Bolivar.

Throughout the year, there are smaller al Parque events dedicated to other musical genres, such as salsa. The event fills up quickly with loud, ruckus dancing and music. It is a fun, exciting way to experience rock n' roll music in Colombia.

There are many other festivals and events in Colombia throughout the year. Once you decide which cities you plan to visit, check out what events may be going on here during the time of year you are visiting. Many festivals are free of charge, and the events are a lot of fun. You can experience Colombian culture with these exciting festivals.

The Hay Festival

Every January in Cartagena, you can attend the Hay Festival. The Hay Festival is an international convention for journalists and literature. There are typically over 180 guests from over 21 countries in attendance. There are several events, workshops, and speakers you can check out. It is a festival that promotes reading and making literature accessible. It helps to bring editors and writers together with readers.

Top 5 Cities
to Visit

Now that we've gone through an overview of Colombia, let's talk about places to stay and things to do. The following five cities are some of the best places to visit. Each city has a lot to offer with historical sites, beautiful architecture, tasty restaurants, and fun things to do around each corner.

If you get a chance to visit all of these cities at some point, you will get to experience the best representations of Colombia. Each city is a testament to the people of the region and their unique experiences within their region.

#1 Bogota

One of the most popular cities to visit in Colombia is its capital—Bogota. In the heart of the Andes Mountains between Monserrate and Guadalupe, this diverse city sits at 2,600 meters above sea level. It is the largest and most booming city in the country. Bogota is considered the melting pot of Colombia. It melds the past with the present with its variety of colonial and modern architecture. It also fuses many different cultures and traditions from around the country into one city.

Bogota was originally a part of the Muisca confederation, which was a group of indigenous chiefs who ruled the area. In 1533, conquistadors were in search of El Dorado as they made it through this region. Gonzalo Jiménez de Quesada established a military encampment in the region. The city became the capital of the country in 1819.

The city is in a savanna region. The average temperature is about 58 °F year round. The city is very modern nowadays and a great place to visit on your journey through the country.

Places to stay

Before you plan your stay, here are some of the top hotels in Bogota. We have included a high-end, mid-range, and budget-friendly option, to meet your travel needs. Whether you are traveling in a group, alone, or as a couple, there are plenty of great places to stay in Bogota.

W. Bogota

https://www.marriott.com/en-us/hotels/bogwh-w-bogota/overview

This luxurious Marriott hotel is an homage to the legend of El Dorado. The hotel is located in the Usaquen neighborhood. The hotel features a bar, 24/7 in-room dining, Wi-Fi, and smart TV. There is a pool, evening entertainment, gym, and spa. Each room is spacious, and the staff are friendly. Around the hotel, there are several restaurants and shops you can visit. This is a pricier hotel, but it mixes traditional Colombian style and hospitality with modern amenities. It is perfect for anyone wanting to stay in a luxury hotel while in Bogota.

Cosmos 100 Hotel

https://www.cosmos100hotel.com/

If you are looking for a mid-priced hotel, the Cosmos 100 Hotel offers over 199 rooms and suites. This hotel is used for business and travel needs. There is a gourmet cafe, 2 bars, and 4 restaurants in the hotel. There is a pool, Finnish sauna, Turkish bath, and Jacuzzi on site. The hotel offers free Wi-Fi. There are room options for however you are traveling—alone, in a group, or as a couple. This is a great option for people looking to get the most bang for their buck.

GHL Hotel Tequendama Bogotá

https://www.tequendamahotel.com/

This budget hotel is located in the center of the city near the most historic sites in Bogota. There is one presidential suite and 87 junior suites on site. The hotel is used for both travel and business. There is a bar, cafeteria, and two restaurants. There is also a spa room. The hotel itself is a bit outdated. The decor and bathrooms could use an update; however, the over quality of service and cleanliness are good for the price.

Things to do

Bogota is a large city, so it may be difficult to decide what to do while there. We have compiled the top 9 experiences you must see in Bogota. There is fun for everyone from children to adults. Whether you are looking for the history of the town or to dive into Colombian culture, there is so much to do and see in Bogota.

1. Discover the historical La Candelaria district

This neighborhood is the historic center of Bogota. Its origins begin with the indigenous tribe the Muiscas, who believed this local was sacred. Then, when the city was founded in 1538, the area took the name of the cathedral that stood there. Now, you can visit several of Bogota's most interesting sites in this historic district.

The Bolero Museum, Luis Angel Arango Library, Garcia Marquez Cultural Center, The Christopher Columbus Theatre, Primatial Cathedral, Chapel of the Tabernacle, and Colonial Arts Museum are all within walking distance in this area.

There are also several local restaurants to visit in this location.

1. View the architecture at the Primatial Cathedral

If you love historical sites and exploring beautiful architecture, Bogota has plenty for you to check out. In Bolivar Square, the first church that was built in Bogota stands. The Primatial Cathedral was erected in 1539. The cathedral has 12 chapels. In the Santa Isabela de Hungria chapel, the remains of Antonio Narino, Gregorio Vásquez de Arce y Ceballos, and Gonzalo Jiménez de Quesada lay to rest. These are important historical figures in Colombian history. Part of the cathedral is shaped like a cross. There are several sculptures around the cathedral.

72

There is a large pipe organ, tons of marble, and Spanish cast bronze. This is a must-see when you travel to Bogota.

2. Check out Casa de Narina

Located in La Candelaria, the historic district in Bogota, the Casa de Narina stands. This is the home and workplace of the Colombian president. The house originally belonged to Antonio Amador José de Nariño y Álvarez del Casal, a leader of independence in the late 1700s. It was later purchased to be the presidential residence. In the 20th century, the house was updated to include neoclassical architecture. Inside the building, there is a hall of flags, paintings of Colombian presidents, and works of art by local artists.

You can book a tour of Casa de Narina, in either Spanish or English. The grounds are intensely guarded, and loitering on the grounds is strictly prohibited.

3. Learn about history and culture at a museum

Bogota has three popular museums to visit: the National Museum of Colombia, The Gold Museum, and The Maloka Interactive Center. Each of these museums offers a glimpse of what life was like in the past and is currently in Colombia.

The National Museum of Colombia has over 20,000 artifacts and works of art. It is located in the former Central Penitentiary.

The Gold Museum has the largest collection of prehistoric goldwork in the world. This museum made National Geographic's list of top museums in the world in 2018. There are over 34,000 pieces of gold in this museum. The legend of El Dorado was born from the ritual of the Muiscas. The museum displays are in both Spanish and English.

In west Bogota, you can visit the Maloka Interactive Center. This is a must-see for families with children visiting the city. There are exhibits kids can interact with covering topics such as science, technology, history, and the universe. Kids will have fun while learning. There are also 3D films shown at the Maloka Interactive Center.

If you are spending several days in Bogota, these museums are the perfect place to visit.

4. Plaza de Bolivar

The 149,650 square foot concrete area is at the heart of Bogota city. Many of the city's municipal buildings, the Primatial Cathedral, the city hall, and the capitol building surround this square. In the Plaza, a monument to Simon Bolivar, the liberator, stands. This important historical figure led Colombia and other South American countries to independence from the Spanish. The square is a place for protests, outdoor vendors, eateries, and live performances.

5. Go shopping in Bogota

There are two great places to shop in Bogota: La Candelaria and La Mercado de las Pulgas de Usaquen. The La Candelaria district has several shops interspersed between the historic sites. This is a great place to do a day trip. You can visit the local shops and get souvenirs while exploring the historic sites of the city.

La Mercado de las Pulgas de Usaquen is an open flea market. You can find food, plants, clothing, jewelry, and artisan crafts sold here. The market is open on Sundays and takes about an hour to walk through and shop. About 300 vendors set up in San Alejo for this weekly market.

6. Party all night

There are several nightclubs that play Latin music. There are several live music venues where you can get drinks and dinner. There are also some local breweries if you want craft beer. Fridays and Saturdays are the wildest nights to explore the city.

Some of the best clubs include Bar la Santa, +57 club, and Sonora Club Bogota. The best bars are Solar Bar, Pravda, Ozzy Company, and Quiebracanto. If you want food with your drinks, try out Colombian Pub, Status Rota Chapinero, Andres D.C., Tramonti, and La Pinta.

7. Take a bike ride through the city

On Sundays and public holidays, you can take a ride down Bogota's cycleway. This is a 75-mile stretch along many of Bogota's main roads. However, on weekdays,

Bogota is heavily congested, and bike riding is much more difficult. You can book a biking tour, which will take you all across the city by historic sites, parks, and barrios to discover the history and culture of the city. These tours start at around $20 per adult. These tours are usually a bit of a challenge, so they are perhaps not the most beginner-friendly. However, this city is well-known for its bike-friendliness, so it is a great way to see the city.

8. Experience the International Bogota Book Fair

In April each year since 1988, Bogota holds a book fair that spans two weeks. Events and training are held to promote reading and books. This is a place for authors, publishers, translators, editors, and book distributors to meet in one place. There are around 270 events held during the book fair each year. There are, of course, thousands of books of every kind to be found at the event. There are book launches, and you can even get signed copies. There are guest speakers.

#2 Medellin

Medellin is the second largest city in Colombia. It sits in the central valley of the Andes Mountains. The city was first a small indigenous village until Mariana of Austria (queen consort) established (1675) the town *Villa de Nuestra Señora de la Candelaria de Medellín*. This is where the name Medellin came from.

Now over 2,000,000 people live in this city. It is the capital of the Antioquia department. In the 19th century, Medellin was known for its exports of gold and coffee. Now, it is renowned for its innovation. The city won the Harvard University Verónica Rudge Urbanism Award for urban development in 2013. This as well as other accolades for urban innovation have been conferred on this city for its initiatives to provide public transportation on a large scale.

The city is also building skyscrapers at high speed, outbuilding Bogota and other cities in Colombia. Medellin's innovation does not stop at transportation and building efforts. They are making strides in research for health care, and there are over 30 universities in the city.

This is truly a city moving at lightning speed into the future, providing an experience worth seeing for yourself.

Places to stay

El Cielo

https://www.elcielohotel.com/

For a luxury experience in Medellin, you can stay at El Cielo. This hotel is located in the quiet Poblado area of Medellin. Here you will find comfort, luxury, and good service. There is a fine dining restaurant on location with a Michelin-star chef. The hotel also features a small sun deck, pool, and gym. It is considered one of the nicest hotels in Medellin. This boutique hotel is beautiful with modern decor, inviting plant walls, and the suites have comfortable furnishings with private baths.

The Charlee Lifestyle Hotel

https://www.thecharlee.com/en/thecharlee/

If you want a unique but more mid-range hotel experience, the Charlee Lifestyle Hotel is a great choice. This hotel has a little bit of everything. Breakfast is included in the price. There is a full sized gym and a rooftop bar and restaurant with a live DJ. There is also an aquarium-style pool. Some of the rooms feature hot tubs. You can have massages in your room, and the decor is modern and spacious. This is a really great place to spend your vacation relaxing before a day (or night) exploring the city.

Hotel BH El Poblado

https://www.bhhoteles.com/bh-el-poblado

Hotel BH El Poblado is a more economic boutique hotel in Medellin. It is located across from the subway, so you can have easy access to transport around the city. There are 70 rooms in the hotel with free Wi-Fi. There is an onsite gym and a delicious breakfast. This is a smaller hotel located on a steep hill, but it is in a quiet and safe neighborhood in Medellin. The rooms are spacious, clean, and modern with hot water.

Things to do

1. Ride the Metrocable

One of the greatest innovations in Medellin is the Metrocable system. This mode of transportation has brought most of the neighborhoods in the city together. The Metrocable is a gondola lift system. These gondolas are able to reach people living on some of the steep hills of the region. There are 16 gondolas along the Metrocable. You can ride them all over the city. The system can carry up to 30,000 people a day. This was one of the first systems of this kind built in South America, but its popularity has spurred other big cities across the continent to install similar transport systems.

You can get a ticket to ride on the Metrocable. It can take you to many parts of the city, or you can ride it up to Parque Arvi for an additional cost.

2. Visit Parque Arvi

Parque Arvi is a large ecological park in the rural area of Medellin. It is a popular tourist attraction. The park covers over 39,000 acres of land and there are 33 miles of walking trails. Parque Arvi comprises 5 smaller parks. There are antique buildings; unique species of flowers, birds, and butterflies; gardens; and shops in this park.

You can hike the walking trails and explore history then purchase cakes, coffee, and crafts from local vendors. If you prefer, you can also picnic in the park, just make sure to clean up after yourself. There are 12 trails, each taking about an hour or two to hike, so the visit to Parque Arvi could take a whole day on your trip to Medellin.

3. Enjoy nature at the Botanical Gardens

With over 4,500 species of flowers and over 1,000 species of wildlife, the Botanical Gardens at the center of Medellin is a beautiful way to spend an afternoon. Entry is free, so this excursion is friendly to your wallet. You can picnic here and enjoy some quiet time away from the busy city.

4. Have fun at Parque Explora

This interactive science museum has over 300 interactive activities that will entertain adults and children alike. It also features the largest freshwater aquarium in South America. In addition, there is a dinosaur exhibit, restaurant, 3D movie theater, and souvenir shop for families to explore.

Parque Explora is a great venue for people looking to spend a family-fun day. But, it is interesting enough for an adult on their own, too.

The aquarium alone is worth the visit. There are 29 tanks with over 300 species of freshwater fish in them. There are also exhibits with reptiles and amphibians to see. You could easily spend a whole day at Parque Explora.

5. Begin the nightlife at Parque Lleras

By day, this park is a small area where you can pick up some local art from vendors. By night, this is the place to begin your excursion through the city. Surrounding the park are bars, restaurants, clubs, and hostels. Natives and tourists alike gather in the park to drink and begin the festivities. Then, they head off to the clubs for some salsa dancing.

Rio Sur also has some nightclubs and bars you can visit if you are in the area.

6. Get a bird's eye view of the city

If you love adventure tourism, you can paraglide through Medellin. The mountainous terrain of the city makes it perfect for riding the thermal currents. Guides will ensure you are safe as you enjoy the beauty of the Andes Mountains from up high.

There are some other options for adventure tourism in Medellin, including riding bikes or ATVs outside of the city.

7. Watch a futbol game

Medellin is home to two futbol clubs: Atlético Nacional and Independiente Medellín. You will want to purchase your tickets in advance to get good seats. The energy in the stadium is electric. Colombians love futbol, and if it is a particularly competitive game, the crowds will go wild.

8. Check out the Museo de Arte Moderno Medellin

This museum is a place for Latin American and Colombian modern artists to show off their work. You can see paintings, sculptures, 3D models, and much more. There are permanent and temporary exhibits you can visit. The building itself is a work of art, with an interesting architectural design. You can visit the restaurant downstairs and climb to the terrace for a view of the city. There is also a souvenir shop and a theater where movies are sometimes shown.

9. Socialize at Mercado del Rio

With over 40 restaurants, this food court is a great place to get a variety of dishes and to socialize with the locals. Mercado del Rio is a lively place near the Museo de Arte Moderno. It is usually teeming with guests during the lunch and dinner rush hours. You can get Mexican, sushi, vegan, cocktails, beers, and much more.

10. Go shopping

If you are looking to shop in Medellin, there are a few options. You can visit El Hueco for street vendors. You can haggle for odds and ends.

For a more traditional shopping experience, you can go to the Centro Commercial Santa Fe. This is a mall with lots of local and international chains inside.

You can also go to Rio Sur for high-end boutiques.

#3 Cali

The third most populated city in Colombia is Santiago de Cali, or Cali for short. Cali is the largest urban city in the south, with a Pacific coast port. Cali was founded by Sebastian Belalcazar in 1536. The area was inhabited by indigenous tribes, but it was outside the Incan empire, so the conquistador was able to claim the area for his own.

At first, Cali was a small port town, but with the establishment of a market plaza and public transportation, the city began to grow. The Pan American

Games were established in 1971 to encourage peace and tranquility in a city where upheaval had been the norm. Soon, the games made Cali the Sports Capital of Colombia.

There are many cultural and historical attractions that draw tourists to this city each year. Cali is located in the Cuaca Valley near the Farallones de Cali (steep hills). The eastern part of the city borders the Cuaca River. The Western Mountain Range sits to the West.

The city enjoys spring-like temperatures throughout the year, but there is some variation between the northern and southern parts of the city due to topography.

The city is not only the third largest in population; it is also the second largest in size. There are a lot of things to do and see here.

Where to stay

Acquasanta Lofts Hotel

This small, boutique hotel has 9 spacious rooms. These rooms have floor-to-ceiling windows, letting in loads of light. There is a jacuzzi on the terrace and a restaurant next door. The service is friendly and clean. It is located in the trendy and quiet part of Cali. There is a nice pool and an espresso machine with delicious, special-blend coffee. This is a great luxury hotel with a small, cozy feel.

Movich Casa de Alferez

https://www.movichhotels.com/en/about-us/

This is a sustainable and modern hotel chain that prides itself on authentic service. The hotel is located in Granada, a popular district for tourism in Cali. The hotel is 9 km from the airport and 5 minutes from downtown. Breakfast is included in the price. There is free Wi-Fi and a gym. This is a midrange-priced hotel that is comfortable, convenient, and has friendly staff.

Ibis Cali Granada

This pet-friendly hotel is perfect for those traveling on a tight budget. It offers comfort and a great location at a low cost. The hotel features Wi-Fi, air conditioning, free parking, and a restaurant and bar. The rooms are comfortable and safe. The breakfast is delicious. It is located near many of the tourist attractions in southern Cali.

What to do

1. Walk the purrfect path

Cali has a cat park along the northern side of the Rio Cali. This park has one, a large bronze statue of a cat sculpted by Hernando Tejada. Since its inception, the park has grown to include 15 statues of cats created by local artists. Surrounding the area are several local ice cream vendors where you can pick up a sweet treat. There are plenty of shady areas for you to rest and biking lanes you can ride along. This is a great leisurely afternoon excursion.

2. Awe at the Church of the Vera Cruz

The neo-Gothic church sits in the center of the city. This bright white cathedral's architectural style stands out amongst the cityscape. The interior is as white as the outside with gold detailing. There are several beautiful statues within the church. It is a popular tourist attraction and can be quite busy during the daytime.

3. See El Cristo Rey

Similar to the statue in Rio, El Cristo Rey is a 26-meter-high statue of Christ. This less famous statue is placed on the Cerros del los Cristales. This hill is rich in quartz deposits, lending it its name. The statue is a commemoration of the 50th anniversary of the end of the War of a Thousand Days. This statue is made of iron and concrete. It weighs 464 tons and was sculpted by Gerardo Navia Carvajal. You can visit this monument for free. There are even some vendors set up around the location where you can get refreshments.

4. Visit the Cali Zoo

The Cali Zoo has over 2,500 animals and 7 exhibits with native species from Colombia and South America. They also have animals from all over the world, including an Australian exhibit with kangaroos. The zoo is located on the west side of the city near the Cali River. There are several trails you can walk along as you explore each exhibit. The trails feel like you are walking in the jungle with all of the native plants and fish ponds along the trails. Iguanas and peacocks roam freely throughout the zoo. The zoo is kept clean and organized. The animals are well treated, and the zoo comes highly recommended by other tourists. This is a great place to take the family or to spend a day checking out the local wildlife while visiting the city.

5. Shop at Galeria Alameda

If you like to shop at local street markets, Galleria Alameda is a place in Cali for street vendors. There are locals selling crafts, food, vegetables, and exotic fruits, flowers, and meats. There are also a lot of food vendors in the area, so you can try out street food. It's a great place to immerse yourself in the culture of Cali.

6. Check out Plaza de Cayzedo

This is the main square of the city of Cali. There is a statue of the local independence martyr Joaquín de Caicedo y Cuero in the center of the square. Surrounding it are important buildings such as the Cathedral of San Pedro. The cathedral is a baroque-style temple with loads of arches, pilasters, and columns. There are domes, a bell tower, and even a large, tubular organ. It is considered a national monument and an asset of national cultural interest.

Also, among the buildings surrounding the square, is the National Palace. This is the home of the Sectional Council of the Judiciary, the Administrative Court of Valle del Cauca, and the Superior Court of Cali. The palace consists of 5 floors with a total of 28 offices. There is also a small museum attached dedicated to sugar cane. This is considered a national monument.

The Edificio Otero is another national monument in Plaza de Cayzedo. The building was built to resemble buildings in Europe. The upper floors functioned as a hotel for a time. The bottom floor became a restaurant. The building was set to be demolished but was declared a national monument in 1977. In 1984, however, a terrible tragedy occurred where 9 people were killed within the building. But, in 2009, the space was recovered and turned into bank offices. You can see the building from the square.

Plaza de Cayzedo is a great place to see historic buildings. There are also several street vendors where you can get a coffee or a souvenir while in the area.

7. Amuse yourself at the museums

There are several museums in Cali you can visit. The Museo de la Caña de Azúcar is dedicated to sugar cane, the crop that has sustained this department. Christopher Columbus introduced sugar cane to the Americas, and the Valle del Cauca turned out to be the perfect mixture of fertile land and perfect conditions to allow this crop to thrive. When visiting this museum, you can learn about the rich history and impact sugar cane has had on Colombia's growth.

If you enjoy modern art, you can check out Museo La Tertulia. This museum has both indoor and outdoor spaces. It features a variety of local art. It's a place to educate others about art and to provide easy access to art for all.

For people who enjoy learning about aerospace, Museo Aereo Fenix is a great museum to visit. Here there is an extensive collection of aircraft, aviation engines, and flight suits. There is also a cafeteria, modeling workshop, and souvenir shop. This place is open to students who are eager to learn about aircraft, but it is also a must-see for those interested in history and airplanes.

8. Dance salsa

Cali is where salsa dancing was born. Salsa music is piped throughout the city. Around Christmas and New Year's, there are salsa parades. At other times of the year, you can visit most nightclubs in the city to dance salsa. There are often famous live performers in the city. If you don't feel confident in your salsa abilities, try taking a salsa lesson. It's fun and gives you a first-hand experience of Cali's rich culture. You can check out the local salsa clubs such as La Topa, MalaMana, and Punto Bare. Everyone dances salsa—locals and tourists alike. It is one of the main attractions in Cali.

9. Get a workout hiking to Las Tres Cruces

According to legend, a demon cursed Cali. Supposedly, some friars placed three bamboo crosses on the hill, and this kept the demon at bay. But, the crosses had to be renewed each year to imprison the demon. Eventually, the more sturdy crosses that now reside on the hill were put into place, trapping the demon permanently.

To get to the hill of the three crosses, first, go to the Normandia neighborhood. Here you will hike a steep hill of over 480 meters to the monument. This hill is a hard trek and there is little shade along the hike. However, there is a lovely view once you reach the top.

10. Enjoy the beauty of Andoke

Andoke is a beautiful park where you can see butterflies. You have to make reservations in advance, but the place is spectacular. There are at least 15 species of native butterflies, trails, and beautiful gardens. You can sit at the cafe with a cup of coffee and empanada and enjoy the serenity of the gardens. There is a map of Colombia in stone. An average visit lasts 1–2 hours, and the park is not far from the Cristo de Rey monument, so you could travel to both locations in one day.

#4 Barranquilla

On the Caribbean side of Colombia, the fourth largest city sits. This is a port city in the delta region of the Magdalena River. Barranquilla is nicknamed "Colombia's Golden Gate." The port city has been a spot for immigrants to enter the country. At its earliest, this is where European settlers docked. After the World Wars, Asian and Middle East, immigrated to the city.

Barranquilla was not established in a pre-Colombian town or founded during the Spanish colonization. Instead, it was a place where native Indians brought supplies to trade. It sprung up from the farm of Nicholas de Barros. He let his workers build homes on the property to support their families until it grew into a town. The town was officially established in 1813.

The city is hot and humid year-round. There are a lot of low-lying areas that can flood during the rainy season.

Barranquilla is a modern city, well-known for its large festivities during Carnival. It is also the home of aviation. The first airline in South America was established in this city.

There are lots to see and do in this city. It is a great place to visit along the Caribbean coast.

Where to stay
Crowne Plaza Barranquilla

https://www.ihg.com/crowneplaza/hotels/us/en/barranquilla/baqbc/hoteldetail

The Crowne Plaza is a chain, luxury hotel with 13 floors of rooms. It is located 39 minutes from the Ernesto Cortissoz Airport and within a large shopping district in Barranquilla. The hotel offers a fitness room, swimming pool, steam room, and a restaurant. This is a dependable company with plenty of good reviews for cleanliness and friendly staff. It is a good choice for someone who wants a comfortable, modern hotel experience.

BH Barranquilla

https://www.bhhoteles.com/bh-barranquilla

For a more romantic experience in Barranquilla, you can check out this boutique hotel. It is located in Prado Alto near several shopping centers, restaurants, and bars. The nightlife is active around this area of town. The interior design is inspired by the Caribbean. There is free Wi-Fi, air conditioning, a jacuzzi, a gym, and over 64 rooms available. Breakfast is included in the cost. The hotel is within walking distance of many of the most popular tourist sites. This is a great hotel for someone who wants convenience and a smaller, cozier hotel experience.

Ibis Barranquilla

If you are staying in Barranquilla on a budget, the Ibis hotel chain is a clean and comfortable place you can stay. The rooms are spartan, but provide everything you need. A breakfast buffet is included in the price. There is free Wi-Fi, a bar area, child-friendly spaces, and it is pet friendly. If you want a comfortable stay for an affordable price, this is the hotel for you.

What to do

1. Visit Bocas de Ceniza

Where the Magdalena River meets the Caribbean Sea, you can find immeasurable beauty. It is a long walk and kind of tricky to get to. Many travelers advise you to hire a guide to take you on a bike or for someone to accompany you on the journey. The road takes you through a very poor part of the town. You can take the train, which there are several negative reviews of, or you can hire an Uber, taxi, or drive yourself. These seem to be the better options. If you walk the long trail, it will take you about 45 minutes. Those who have made the trek say it is worth it.

On the other hand, sometimes you can rent a boat or get on a guided boat tour of the area, which is a much nicer way to experience the convergence of the river and the sea.

2. Visit the Barranquilla Zoo

This zoo is smaller than the one in Cali, but it still has 550 animals including the manatee, the eagle, the condor, and the spectacled bear. You can even touch some of the animals at this zoo. There is a cafe you can visit with drinks and empanadas. It's a great place to take kids for a couple of hours during the daytime in Barranquilla.

3. Enjoy the sunny beaches

Playa del Salgar is about 15 minutes outside of the city near the Villa Alcatraz. You can relax under umbrellas and eat at the local restaurants. It is a popular beach perfect for a family vacation. While there, you can also visit El Castillo del Salgar, which is a monument with a restaurant located within it. It was a fort built up to protect the port. It is used mainly as an event space now. You can also take surfing lessons here.

Another noteworthy beach in the area is Sabanilla Beach. It is a 5 km stretch of beachline where huts and restaurants line the area. It is a popular place to visit while in Barranquilla. This space offers a pretty traditional beach-going experience for those wanting to spend some hours in the sun.

4. Check out the Museo Romantico

If you want to learn more about the history of Barranquilla, this museum is a great place to start. The museum is located inside an 18th-century building and is loaded with artifacts. Some of the items include letters from Simon Bolivar and past costumes worn during Carnival. This small but unique museum is worth a look if you are a history lover.

5. View the Queen Mary Cathedral

In the center of Barranquilla, on the western side of Plaza de Paz, sits the Catedral Metropolitana María Reina de Barranquilla. It took 27 years for this cathedral to be constructed. It was designed by an Italian architect. This modernist-style building is 4,274 square meters in area. It is considered a cultural landmark.

6. Watch a futbol game

The World Cup qualifying famous Atlético Junior and the Colombia National Teams play at Roberto Meléndez Metropolitan Stadium. You can buy tickets in advance and get good seats. You can cheer along with crowds of fans. This is the perfect outing for a family, individual, or group. You can enjoy the energy of the fans whether you are a futbol fan or just a casual spectator.

7. Walk along the Gran Malecon

For 5 km along the west bank of the Magdalena River, there is a large boardwalk called the Golden Gate Park. There are restaurants, shops, and cultural events to see and visit as you walk the Malecon. You can also play sports at fields and parks located across the stretch. Live bands perform. You can see boats as they pull into the river. It is a beautiful and lively experience when you visit Barranquilla.

8. Attend the Carnival

In late February, if you visit Barranquilla, the main attraction will be Carnival, a festival that occurs at the onset of Lent. Barranquilla's Carnival Festival is the second largest in the world. If you travel to the city during this time, you won't be able to miss the lively music, dancing, drinking, and celebrating. The costumes are bold and eccentric. The spirits are high and full of excitement. It is an experience to remember. Be aware, though, that the city is very crowded during this season.

9. Explore the parks

Barranquilla is a modern city with plenty of parks to visit. You can visit the new children's play area in Parque Suri Salcedo. This is a great place to let the kids run and play.

Or, you can enjoy the open-air theater in Parque Cultural del Caribe. The Museo de Caribe is also located in this area, which has plenty of cultural exhibits that are fun to explore.

You could also check out Parque Muvdi, which is a great place to enjoy sports such as tennis and volleyball.

10. Take a tour of the city

There are several different ways to tour the city. You can walk in the footsteps of Gabriel Garcia Marquez (a Colombian novelist and screenwriter). You can take a guided, four-hour tour through the city from the entrance of the Museo de Caribe. You can also take a 6-hour tour of the Gran Malecon, the Downtown area, and the Carnival museum. If you want to try out the flavors of Barranquilla, consider a food tour. Finally, you can also get a tour of the Tayrona National Park, which is about 2 hours from Barranquilla.

#5 Cartegena

One of the most popular cities in Colombia is Cartagena. This northern port city was historically an important trade route. During Spanish rule, this port shipped silver out of the country to Spain and imported African slaves.

The city is located between two strategic rivers: the Magdalena River and the Sinu River. Prior to the Spanish conquest, Cartagena was the home of the oldest dated human civilization in Colombia. This civilization was thriving here as early as 4000 BC. Before the Spanish arrived, several indigenous peoples dwelled in this region. By the early 1500s, the Spanish had infiltrated this area.

The city built extensive walls around itself to keep pirates out, and these walls known as La Heroica, are 11 km of stone that took 200 years to erect.

Cartagena has a humid and tropical environment. It is usually quite warm here, with an extensive wet season from May to November. This is still one of the largest ports in South America. It is now a popular tourist location and center of commerce for Colombia.

Where to stay

Hotel Casa San Agustin

https://www.hotelcasasanagustin.com/en/home.html

For a luxurious stay in Cartagena, this hotel has the modern beauty of the Caribbean paired with the appearance of colonial buildings. This boutique hotel has 20 rooms and 11 suites. The white-washed walls have original frescoes and floor-to-ceiling 17th-century wooden beams. The hotel is made up of three buildings. There is an ancient aqueduct featured as the face of this gorgeous hotel. The hotel features an outdoor pool, solarium, terrace with lounge, game room, and pool bar. There is free continental breakfast and Wi-Fi. This is a fantastic place to stay for a relaxing vacation.

Hotel Capellan

https://hotelcapellandegetsemani.com/

For a mid-range priced hotel, Hotel Capellan is an excellent choice. It is located 1,000 feet from Cartagena's Convention Center in the Getsemani neighborhood. The hotel is air-conditioned and has free Wi-Fi, an outdoor pool, and an outdoor garden. Each room has a private bathroom. There is a continental breakfast. It is a comfortable, clean, and friendly hotel located in the heart of Cartagena.

Casa India Catalina

https://www.hotelcasaindiacatalina.com.co/en/?cur =COP

In the walled city of Cartagena, this budget hotel is a comfortable place to stay. It is air-conditioned, has an outdoor swimming pool, and offers free Wi-Fi. From this location, you can travel just 2 miles to the harbor or to Centennial Park. This hotel offers comfort at an affordable price.

What to do

1. Walk through the walled city

In 1984, Cartagena was named a UNESCO World Heritage Site. There are many colonial buildings to check out here. You can enter through the Clock Tower. This is a 30-meter monument built into the wall.

In the city, you can go to the San Pedro Claver Church, which was built in 1580. It was named for Pedro Claver, who came to Cartagena to baptize thousands of people. He was especially dedicated to baptizing slaves. He was named a saint in 1884. Now, there is a museum dedicated to him at the cathedral.

You can also visit the Plaza de Santo Domingo. As funny as it may seem, touching the butt of the statue of Botero in the plaza is said to bring good luck.

There are also a couple of parks in the vicinity you can visit. It is a great place to go. You can spend a whole day in the walled city.

2. Walk through the old city

You can take a free walking tour of the old city, learning the history of the unique architecture. This tour takes about two and a half hours. You can also do paid tours. These tours help you appreciate the long, interesting history of Cartagena and its impact on the people in the town.

3. Dip your toes in the ocean

One of the main attractions of Cartagena is its gorgeous beaches. La Playa Blanca is the most public beach here. The white sands and warm, Caribbean air make this a lovely beach-going experience.

However, if you want to check out Baru, a peninsula with white and pink sands, you can enjoy the ocean through adventure tourism. Here you can see to the bottom of the ocean, where loads of tropical fish dwell. You can surf, dive, water ski, and snorkel here. Not far off, there are mangrove swamps and underwater gardens that are a must-see.

4. Explore the San Felipe Castle

This fortress was built to keep the English from taking control. This castle was built atop San Lazaro hill and completed in 1657. You can wander through the tunnels of the castle and take pictures from the top of the castle. It is now considered one of the 7 wonders of Colombia. It takes about 1 hour to tour the castle.

5. Try the food at the open-air market

There are several places in Cartagena to shop. You go to the Bazurto Market for some local food. This open-air market is a unique experience. In fact, Anthony Bourdain has been here to try the local cuisine. It is an experience you won't quickly forget with lively, loud commotion, and vendors with food of all types all over. It's a great way to experience the culture of the city.

6. Walk through Centenario Park

Between the old city center and Getsemani, there is a large park called Centennial Park. It was built for the 100th-anniversary celebration of Cartagena's independence. You might blink and miss the park, but if you focus closely, you can see monkeys in the trees. Rumors suggest that many of these monkeys were rescued from poachers. There are also sloths there. You can even share a banana with one of these monkeys. It is a neat way to see some wildlife while in Cartagena.

7. Check out the nightlife

You can find it at most local bars and restaurants. You can start out your night at La Plaza de Trinidad to listen to live music and drink a local beer.

The popular alcohol of choice in Colombia is El Aguardiente, but you can find some delightful rum-tasting experiences in Cartagena.

You can also walk along the peninsula to see the night lights and beautiful skyscrapers.

This is a great way to spend a romantic evening or explore the city.

8. See the city from afar

Atop La Popa, the highest hill in Cartagena, you can get an impressive view of the city. Once you reach the top of the hill, you can tour the convent situated at the top. The best way to get to La Popa is via taxi. You could walk, but it is a long journey, and the trek takes you through some poorer communities.

9. Take a boat

You can rent a private boat and travel to Rosario Islands. This is a day trip that takes you to some of the best beaches near Cartagena. Rosario Islands are particularly popular for party-goers.

You can also take a group tour boat to the islands. Even though the boat is crowded, you can dance, sunbathe, and day drink here. Once you get to the islands, you can snorkel and enjoy the day along the beach.

10. Scuba dive to see shipwrecks

Cartagena has a long and old history. There are beautiful coral reefs and shipwrecks you can visit if you are a scuba diver. The best places to scuba dive are the Rosario Islands, Salmedina Shipwrecks, Varadero Reef, Baru, and Tierra Bomba islands. There are a large number of diverse fish and shark species swimming amongst the reefs. You can even get glimpses of octopuses and lobsters after sunset. There are spots for experienced and novice divers alike. Cartagena is a wonderful city to explore the underwater world of the Caribbean Sea.

Frequently
Asked Questions

Here are some answers to questions about Colombia to help you navigate the country during your travels.

Does Colombia have seasons?

No. The country is located on the equator and maintains a similar temperature year-round. There is a rainy season and a dry season. Also, temperatures vary based on the height of the location, rather than the time of year. There are cooler temperatures at higher elevations and warmer near the coast.

The best time to travel to Colombia depends on your purpose. For the best hiking weather, December to February is the best time. For whale-watching, March to November is the best time. To visit the Amazon, October to November is the best time.

Is Colombia safe to travel through?

Colombia has worked tirelessly to improve the safety of travel for tourists in their country. However, there are still some areas that are unsafe to travel to. Always check with the safety guidelines administered by the government before traveling to certain areas. Women traveling alone are also at more risk of danger than other travelers. Use extra caution.

As of right now, the border between Venezuela and Colombia is considered unsafe. Also, try to avoid the Arauca, Cauca, and Norte de Santander departments. You can check the current status of certain areas at the following web address.

https://travel.state.gov/content/travel/en/internati onal-travel/International-Travel-Country-Information-Pages/Colombia.html

The safest places to visit in Colombia currently are Bogota, Medellin, and Cartagena.

Can you drink the water?

Most of the water in large, urban cities in Colombia is fine to drink. In smaller towns, you may need to be more cautious. The rule of thumb is to follow what the locals are doing. If everyone seems to be drinking from a bottle, do the same. If everyone freely drinks from the tap, you can follow suit.

What is transportation like in Colombia?

For the most part, you can travel via taxi, bus, Uber, and airplane (in major cities). There are some places where you will have to rent a boat, such as traveling to an island outside of Cartagena. If you are in a more remote part of the country, airplanes may be harder to come by. The Amazon region still has dirt roads and is difficult to travel through.

Do you tip in Colombia?

Tipping is not customary in Colombia. Most restaurants add a 10% tip to the bill, and taxi drivers don't expect a tip, but if you feel compelled to give one for excellent service, people will gladly accept them.

Is Colombia family-friendly?

Colombia strives to be friendly toward everyone. There are plenty of family-friendly events and locations in the major cities. Zoos, historical sites, and adventure tourist attractions that are aimed toward family groups. The beaches are also a great family-friendly vacation spot.

Is Colombia LGBTQ-friendly?

Although Colombia is one of the more progressive countries in South America, there are still some people who are disapproving. Be cautious, especially at night, in rural areas, or if you are traveling alone.

However, there are some great places that are openly accepting of the LGBTQ community, including some gay bars and Latin America's largest gay club Theatron.

Does Colombia offer vegan or vegetarian options?

In the larger cities, there are restaurants and menu options with vegan and vegetarian options. If you have other dietary restrictions, such as allergies, it is important to let the restaurant staff know in advance. Most places are willing to be accommodating.

Local fruits and vegetables are always a part of the menu, so you can find some more vegetarian-friendly meal options.

What are the most important items to pack?

Of course, don't forget your passport, but in addition to that essential item, remember to bring mosquito repellant, sunscreen, sunglasses, a universal charging cord, waterproof protection for any cameras you bring, and comfortable shoes.

Based on where you are traveling to in Colombia, you will need to wear layers. Mountainous regions can get chilly, especially at night. The coastal regions are generally very hot and humid.

Can you keep contact with home?

If you send a postcard of contact by mail, the mail takes about a month to travel internationally. Calling collect can be expensive, but it is an option if you need to get into contact with family immediately.

Free Wi-Fi is available in most hotels, so you can use apps to communicate with family members.

You will not have cell service on your phone while in Colombia, but you can buy a cheap phone within the country that you can use while on vacation. This will allow you the ability to communicate with others.

What is the currency in Colombia?

Colombian pesos is the currency. It comes in coins as small as 50 COP and can range as large as bills of 50.000 COP. The currency rate is unstable, so before you travel check the current rates. At the moment, $1 USD is about 4908 COP.

You can take out money at ATMs in any of the major cities. You can also use your cards, but make sure your bank knows you are in Colombia, so they don't report your purchases as fraud.

What is the language spoken in Colombia?

Spanish is the main language of the country. There are over 68 languages spoken in the country. There is not a lot of English spoken, except in larger cities.

In larger metropolitan cities, you will be able to get around alright without speaking Spanish, but in smaller villages, it could be more difficult. There are many English translations for guided tours and much more in most big cities, but this is not always the case.

It would be beneficial to know some basic Spanish to help you get around, especially in smaller cities. You may not be able to find anyone who speaks English in these locations.

CONCLUSION

Visiting Colombia is a spectacular experience—from the modern cities to the mountainous terrain to the sunny beaches to the rainforest—there is a little something for everyone. Colombia has a rich and diverse history of conquest and independence. The people are varied and strong. The culture is full of music, art, dancing, and fun.

The varying landscape offers a diverse look at the world. You can see savannas, mangroves, beaches, mountains, cloud forests, and rainforests all in one country. This provides a home to some unique species that are found nowhere else in the world. The country has taken great efforts to preserve the environment with extensive parks and preserves. Colombia is also working to make tourism more eco-friendly.

There are so many great festivals to see, including Barranquilla's Carnival. Each of the major cities has its own sites to see, with rich and vibrant history. There are also many museums and cultural centers where you can truly immerse yourself. The cities are modern and fast-paced, with beautiful landmarks and fun things to do around every corner. The hotels and places to stay will wow you with luxury and impeccable service. Colombia is a fantastic country to spend a few days or an extended vacation because you will be left wanting more.

The food and drinks in Colombia are unrivaled, with dishes full of flavor and regional charm. Many of the ingredients in the dishes are sourced locally, and you will get a chance to try many new fruits and vegetables. Seafood and soup lovers will have a wide array of choices in delectable bites, but also, people who love to grab food from street vendors will find delightful tastes and smells around every corner. And, of course, you cannot forget to grab a cup of coffee while you are here.

You can walk in the footsteps of many historical figures as you look at buildings and monuments that have stood in the same place for hundreds of years. You can even search the depths of the ocean to look at ships, thousands of years under the sea.

You also won't want to pass up local craft vendors and artists, who show how colorful and creative they can be. There are also many boutique shops that sell gorgeous clothing made by local fashion designers and artisans. The garb reflects the vibrancy of the culture throughout the centuries. Not only are Colombians skilled weavers, but carvers and sculptors. You can find many beautiful, hand-hewn statues at local vendors.

Colombia is not only a global powerhouse in coffee and cut flowers, it is a gorgeous home to diverse people full of wonder and beauty. Throughout the years, Colombia has worked hard to make its country a safe and welcoming place to visit. In recent years, tourism has begun to boom, and the Colombian people strive to welcome all to their shores.

On your travels through the country, be sure to take in the scenery, slow down and admire the history, and appreciate the unique charm this country has to offer.

REFERENCES

https://www.worldatlas.com/maps/colombia#:~:text=Colo
mbia%20%28officially%2C%20Republic%20of%20
Colombia%29%20is%20a%20country,Colombia%20
also%20partially%20lies%20in%20the%20Southern
%20hemisphere

https://kids.nationalgeographic.com/geography/countries/a
rticle/colombia

https://www.volcanodiscovery.com/colombia.html#:~:text
=Colombia%20has%2015%20volcanoes%20conside
red%20active.%20The%20volcanoes,plates%2C%20
the%20Nazca%2C%20Caribbean%20and%20South
%20American%20plates

https://thefactfile.org/interesting-facts-colombia/

https://www.otherwayround.travel/interesting-facts-about-
colombia/

https://www.britannica.com/place/Colombia

https://baquianos.com/en/blog/deserts-in-colombia

https://www.colombia.co/en/colombia-
country/environment/fascinating-facts-colombias-
favorite-birds-animals/

https://www.worldatlas.com/articles/native-plants-of-
colombia.html

https://internationalliving.com/colombian-food/

https://www.destinavo.com/en/colombian-food/

https://www.tasteatlas.com/50-most-popular-foods-in-
colombia

https://www.theunconventionalroute.com/colombian-drinks/

https://www.mycolombianrecipes.com/12-traditional-colombian-drinks-you-must-try/

https://medellinguru.com/colombian-drinks/

https://folkcloud.com/folk-music-by-country/colombia

https://www.nationalgeographic.com/travel/slideshow/partner-content-the-rhythm-of-colombia

https://theculturetrip.com/south-america/colombia/articles/the-untold-story-behind-colombias-obsession-with-cycling/

https://www.tripadvisor.com/Attraction_Review-g297473-d4783135-Reviews-Estadio_Metropolitano_Roberto_Melendez-Barranquilla_Atlantico_Department.html

https://www.wbsc.org/en/news/new-national-baseball-stadium-colombia-inaugurated-wbsc-international-friendlies

https://www.racingcircuits.info/south-america/colombia/autodromo-de-tocancipa.html#:~:text=The%20Autodromo%20de%20Tocancip%C3%A1%20is%20Colombia%27s%20only%20active,Six%20Hours%20endurance%20race%20each%20December.%20Active%20Permanent

https://www.touropia.com/best-beaches-in-colombia/

https://southamericabackpacker.com/colombia/taganga/

https://whc.unesco.org/en/list/1216/

https://www.parquesnacionales.gov.co/portal/en/ecotourism/pacific-region/malpelo-flora-and-fauna-sanctuary/

https://whc.unesco.org/en/list/1174/

https://www.kuodatravel.com/national-parks-in-colombia/#1_Tayrona

https://www.thebrokebackpacker.com/festivals-in-colombia/

https://www.historyhit.com/locations/plaza-de-bolivar/

https://colombia.travel/en/bogota

https://www.historyhit.com/locations/casa-de-narino/

https://www.tripadvisor.com/Attraction_Review-g294074-d1382992-Reviews-Mercado_de_las_Pulgas_de_Usaquen-Bogota.html

https://www.nightflow.com/bogota-nightlife/

https://www.tripadvisor.com/SmartDeals-g294074-Bogota-Hotel-Deals.html

https://medellinguru.com/parque-arvi/

https://www.thecrazytourist.com/25-best-things-to-do-in-medellin-colombia/

https://medellinguru.com/parque-explora/

https://www.thecrazytourist.com/25-best-things-to-do-in-medellin-colombia/

https://www.tripadvisor.com/SmartDeals-g297478-Medellin_Antioquia_Department-Hotel-Deals.html

https://www.tripadvisor.com/Hotel_Review-g297475-d4156740-Reviews-AcquaSanta_Lofts_Hotel-Cali_Valle_del_Cauca_Department.html

https://www.tripadvisor.com/SmartDeals-g297475-Cali_Valle_del_Cauca_Department-Hotel-Deals.html

https://www.tripadvisor.com/Hotel_Review-g297475-d13520312-Reviews-Ibis_Cali_Granada-Cali_Valle_del_Cauca_Department.html

https://www.atlasobscura.com/places/cat-park-parque-el-gato-de-tejada

https://www.zoologicodecali.com.co/copia-de-home

https://www.colombia.com/turismo/sitios-turisticos/cali/atractivos-turisticos/sdi212/53339/museo-de-la-cana-de-azucar

https://museolatertulia.com/visitanos/

https://discoverdiscomfort.com/best-cali-salsa-clubs/

https://www.tripadvisor.com/Attraction_Review-g297475-d6966718-Reviews-Mariposario_Andoke-Cali_Valle_del_Cauca_Department.html

https://www.tripadvisor.com/SmartDeals-g297473-
        Barranquilla_Atlantico_Department-Hotel-
        Deals.html

https://pueblospatrimoniodecolombia.travel/playas-en-
        barranquilla/#Playa_Puerto_Salgar

https://colombia.travel/en/barranquilla

https://www.barranquilla.gov.co/cultura/con-mas-de-10-
        millones-de-visitantes-el-gran-malecon-del-rio-
        consolida-su-atractivo-turistico

https://www.thecrazytourist.com/15-best-things-to-do-in-
        barranquilla-colombia/

https://colombia.travel/en/cartagena/walls-cartagena

https://www.cartagenaexplorer.com/where-to-stay-best-
        areas-to-stay-cartagena-colombia-guide/

https://www.cartagenaexplorer.com/where-to-stay-best-
        areas-to-stay-cartagena-colombia-guide/

https://www.cartagenaexplorer.com/visitors-guide-san-
        pedro-claver-church-cartagena/

https://www.kimkim.com/c/planning-your-visit-to-
        colombias-amazon-region

https://www.hayfestival.com/

https://www.goway.com/travel-information/central-and-
        south-america/colombia/colombia-faqs/

https://www.vagabondjourney.com/where-you-can-drink-
        tap-water-in-colombia/

https://medellinliving.com/how-to-buy-use-cell-phones-
        colombia/#:~:text=You%20can%20also%20buy%2
        0cell%20phones%20through%20mobile,of%20the%
        20malls%20in%20the%20cities%20in%20Colombia

https://lulocolombia.travel/faq/#1606264741920-7b51089f-
        cc18

https://www.lonelyplanet.com/articles/best-time-to-visit-
        colombia

https://www.worldhistory.org/El_Dorado/

https://theculturetrip.com/south-
        america/colombia/articles/the-mystery-behind-the-
        lake-of-fools-gold-colombia/

https://www.britannica.com/place/Colombia/The-arts

https://www.colombia.co/en/colombia-country/famous-people-from-colombia/colombian-top-fashion-designers-that-should-be-on-your-radar/

https://www.colombia.co/en/colombia-culture/art/art/

https://www.colombia.co/en/colombia-country/famous-people-from-colombia/the-colombian-film-industry-each-time-closer-to-the-oscars/

Made in the USA
Las Vegas, NV
03 September 2023

76964294R00069